FAREWELL, MY LOVELIES

Farewell, My Lovelies

poems by Diann Blakely

Story Line Press

SLP

Published by Story Line Press, Three Oaks Farm, PO Box 1240, Ashland, OR
97520-0055
www.storylinepress.com

This publication was made possible thanks in part to the generous support of
the Nicholas Roerich Museum, the Andrew W. Mellon Foundation, the Na-
tional Endowment for the Arts, and our individual contributors.

Book design by Lysa McDowell
Cover photograph by Skip Jackson and Michael Whitehead
Cover hat is loaned from the collection of Alice Randall and
Caroline Randall Williams
Back cover, author photo by Robin Haney

Printed in Canada

Library of Congress Cataloging-in-Publication Data

Blakely, Diann, 1957– Farewell, my lovelies: poems / by Diann Blakely
p. cm.
ISBN 1-885266-83-9 (alk. paper)
I. Title.

PS3552.L35F37 2000
811'.54—dc21   99-55821

ACKNOWLEDGMENTS

Boulevard: "Wilde and Pasolini in Heaven"
Colorado Review: "Multiple Exposure"
Columbia: "Chorale"
Denver Quarterly: "Bodies," "Yucatan, November"
Harvard Magazine: "The Storm" (reprinted in *The Prague Revue*)
Homeworks: An Anthology of Tennessee Writers: "The Cemetery Book of Caroline McGavock"
Louisville Review: "Birmingham, 1962" reprinted in *Pushcart Prize Anthology XIX*, also *Reading Our Lives: Alabama Writers*
Michigan Quarterly Review: "Jehovah Jiveh," and "Reunion Banquet, Class of '79" (reprinted in *Lights, Camera, Poetry!* ed. Jason Shinder; the *The Movies,* eds. Laurence Goldstein and Ira Konigsberg)
The Nation: "Christmas Call"
New Letters: "Magi"
The Paris Review: "The Dolls"
Ploughshares: "Foucault in Vermont," "*The Homeless in America*"
Prairie Schooner: "Duplex Noir"
Poetry East: "Halloween"
Shenandoah: "Descant," "Hound Dog"
The Southern Review: "Delta Funeral," "History," "Story Hour"
Third Coast: "Tonsillectomy"
Verse: "The Old Slave Market"

"Wilde and Pasolini in Heaven" is for David St. John. "Jehovah Jiveh" is for LH. "The Old Slave Market, Charleston" is for Greg Flowers.

For their friendship and careful reading of these poems, I wish to thank Molly Bendall, Ben Downing, Frank Gaspar, Mark Jarman, the late Bill Matthews Preston Merchant, Margaret Renkl, and Bill Wadsworth. And very special thanks to Robert McDowell.

For my parents,

In Memory of Lynda Hull and William Matthews

TABLE OF CONTENTS

I

Last Dance / 15
The Storm / 17
The Cemetery Book of Caroline McGavock / 18
Halloween / 20
Wilde and Pasolini in Heaven / 22
Birmingham, 1962 / 23
Reunion Banquet, Class of '79 / 25
Foucault in Vermont / 27
Duplex Noir / 28
Yucatan, November / 30

II

Delta Funeral / 35
Independence Day / 38
23 Johnson Avenue, 1985 / 40
Magi / 41
The Dolls / 43
Tonsillectomy / 44
All Those Pretty Ones / 46
Jehovah Jiveh / 47
Christmas Call / 49
Prodigals / 51

III

Descant / 55
History / 57
The Old Slave Market, Charleston / 58
Hound Dog / 60
Georgia Pilgrimage / 62
"The Homeless in America" / 64
Multiple Exposure / 66
Bodies / 67
Story Hour / 70
Chorale / 72

I

LAST DANCE

Not swans or flowers, these tulle-shrouded furies gliding
    en pointe, their eyes blank in chignonned heads that tilt
        as each glances at the hand curved on her breast,

black-lipsticked mouths hardened as the eyes shift toward
    Myrthe, their merciless queen, who tells them *yes,*
        Albrecht too, though his clasped hands beg forgiveness,

love's betrayers must be danced to death, leapt
    and spun till blood cools in his veins. That when tenderness
        ghost-flickers those hollows where their hearts once beat,

they must look at that cradled air and remember
    the babies denied them. Merciless, their black lips curl
        as Myrthe flings Albrecht to his first unearthly partner,

then pirouettes offstage as *Giselle*'s starring bad-ass.
    Acting ugly, said my family's women when I squirmed
        at concert halls like this, itchy in lace skirts,

or tantrummed during yearly perms. *Acting ugly,*
    they'd say about these red-lipped girls in the bathroom
        at intermission, blowing smoke and admiring

each other's baby doll dresses, worn with fishnets
    by the taller, whose peroxide-stricken curls droop
        to her shoulders. *A fucking bore,* she pronounces

the ballet, slumps regally against the tiled wall,
    a fucking A-1 bore. Their mothers bought the tickets,
        bargaining seats for Hole's next concert, I hear too,

and through smoke glance at the black armband—*Kurt Forever*—
    tied to the blond queen's sleeve. We both saw his widow
        on TV, screaming to mourners in phrases mostly bleeped,

her darkly-painted mouth condemning the ugliest act
    she'd known—her husband's hand caressing his own temple
        with a gun's cold and blue-sheened barrel after years

of their ghost-dance with heroin; and how they wanted
    to fly higher than bodies lifted in roiling pits,
        than those guitars' amped keening snarl: *Kurt Forever*

and never again—*an asshole, a fucker*—formed
    by the lipsticked mouth before footage cut to stills
        of their child, eyes blank as the lamb's propped beside her,

lips parted wide while her blond mother tried to hush
    that merciless birth-wail, that transcendent fury
        thumping loud and echoed in tiny blood-leaping veins.

THE STORM

Why shouldn't I stay, whispered part of myself—
He'd stocked plenty of groceries for three,
Maybe four days. Red wine too, a whole case.
The ice, like a bright skin, had covered the trees
And main road to the nearest town. A wreck,
The car crashed, was what I imagined—there
Were things I feared more than adulterous sex.
And he'd touched me already, kissed my hair
And chapped lips: how much further could I fall?
Winds howled an old answer and I thought of
Francesca, swirling in that second circle.
Life wasn't bad, for hell. Whispering *love*—
But not just for one night—through those great gusts
Of wind, God, shouldn't she have been pleased?

THE CEMETERY BOOK
OF CAROLINE MCGAVOCK

—Carlton House, Franklin, Tennessee

Gathered like rumors, clouds hung close
to the ground, whitened each dawn with frost.
When the battle started, she thought she heard thunder
then remembered the season and three past years
of war, remembered the scouts she'd let sleep
on her rugs. A prayer to the God of Calvin

her forebears brought with them from Ulster
came next; she knew will was damnation
and all things predestined, and yet protested
as she had her firstborn's last fever,
his sister's choking on phlegm, the cousin and brother
who'd limped home that month, one missing a leg,

the other three toes to frostbite, also an eye.
By afternoon, more than two thousand lay dead,
twice that wounded, five generals shrouded
on her porch. The children huddled downcellar
with the few house servants who had claimed
they were too old for freedom, hoping to die

where they'd lived, raised young ones
their own. They trusted in prayer, having prayed
for years not to be sold from their families.
When the surgeon cried for more hands
than she had, she brought Gabriel and Susie upstairs.
The nursery they'd tended that morning was a riot

of bodies, strewn toys soaked from the blood
that spurted with each scalpel-cut
through sinew and tendon, severing shattered arms
and legs, the hands or feet of the luckier.
The walls themselves seemed to bleed; the horror
of splintered bone protruding from a length of flesh

she couldn't name as the surgeon reached out
the window and dropped it two stories below.
I stand at a glass case, examining pages
yellowed and speckled as the linens spread
without wrinkle on the four-posters upstairs.
Mass graves were the norm then; too many to dig

separate holes for, not enough men left to dig them.
And they had to hurry: the ground, though warmed
by puddles of blood, would harden with frost
at nightfall. After the final surrender,
what kind of help did she have, reclaiming bodies
from Tennessee soil, checking their pockets

for letters or inscribed photographs, anything
to tell her those names? Each was reburied alone,
a limestone slab etched with a cross
stating all she'd learned. At night, both children
beside her, she knelt on this floor,
still dark with stain over a hundred years later.

HALLOWEEN

Clutching nearly-full bags, they knock at my door,
the last on a block I moved to this summer,
their high-pitched voices hoarse in chill night air;
the youngest, whose short legs haven't walked long

without a mother's steadying hand, are tired.
I'm tired from my walk too, & still clad in sweaty
black spandex, stepping over piles of unshelved books
& month-old student papers to greet vampires,

a purple dinosaur, & two floral-sheeted ghosts.
They probably live nearby, but on power-strides
through the neighborhood, my ragged panting's clash
with the Walkman's beat, also the weights that threaten

to slide from my thin wrists, are distraction enough:
I don't recognize even the kids without masks,
bending to offer shrink-wrapped boxes of raisins,
which some examine suspiciously, peeling off

their mittens to finger-test the seals. A ghost
looks back at her mother, who swaps half-waves with me;
once I'd have thought the worried scrutiny creasing
her forehead rude, but what news-watcher can blame

such stares these days? Close to midnight, I find a few
last chocolates, but I lost my sweet tooth
a decade ago, after high school's late talks fueled
with Chips Ahoy & Goodbars on marriage, kids too;

after college's on poems, consciousness-raising,
sometimes the Rolling Stones, while washing down
hash-laced brownies with rum-&-Tabs. Now my third glass
of red wine spills across pages dimly wreathed

by cigarette smoke: post-modern blasphemy, sure,
these perverse habits, but ones affecting
my own body, though the Puritans shunned neighbors,
even hanged them as witches, for less; in Europe,

such women were burned & their ashes buried
at crossroads, folk believing passersby's feet
would keep these souls confined to earth, from gathering
in woods as they'd done when alive, to chant

in black rhythms & copulate with animals.
Or each other. Or the Devil, offering cups
of blood, babies too, probably not theirs,
moste beeing barren, my old textbook says,

some drinkinge foulé potions to bringe on stillbirthes
& unholie abortions; the sacrifices
made when full moons like this one rose, enlarged
& dazzling in the glass framing the door. Tonight

she too is less sisterly than maternal, orange
& thick-bellied, flaring tree limbs skeletal as mine
while they sing harshly in the almost-winter wind,
while she dims the few stars fixed around her.

WILDE AND PASOLINI IN HEAVEN

At first, they'll eye each other warily:
Oscar's ruffled cuffs and velvet waistcoat
Seem to scorn, by their Bond Street tailoring,
Pa's tight rayon pants stuffed into cheap boots,
The nylon shirt lurid as Rome's Circus
Or his beloved Pontormos, now displayed
Behind two layers of shatterproof glass.
Gabriel's the go-between, back from forays
To earth, like that garden talk with Mary—
One glance and Oscar's arched brow is levelled;
Pa gulps his jokes about fat British arses
And their queen. Devoted but bickering friends
As years pass: "Each man kills the thing he loves . . ."
"*Basta*—that sweet punk made tire-ruts my grave."

BIRMINGHAM, 1962

Scarcely affluent, we always had maids.
    One worked a few months then left for Detroit,
the next for a husband's hometown; some took
    their children and returned to elderly mothers
who still lived beneath rural tin roofs,
    having found cities and their men "no good."
I was a good girl, they all told me so
    when I'd stand by their ironing boards, dipping
my fingers in a bowl of water to sprinkle

on my father's shirts, my mother's lace-wristed
    blouses, the pale dresses I wore to church.
The TV murmured with husky-voiced women
    in negligees; I was admonished to listen
to what preachers told me, to remember
    that Jesus was watching always. I watched
black hands guiding roasts out of ovens,
    turning pieces of chicken in skillets
of sizzling oil, noticed the rough pink

of blisters and scars. These hands dressed me
    each morning; I imagined they loved me.
One August afternoon, my mother home late,
    back from a bridge party, shopping. Delores
had missed the last bus. We drove for miles
    through heat-steaming streets to a part of town
I'd never been to; the houses grew smaller
    and closer together. Peeling paint.
No real driveways, or yards. Then nothing

but rows of small brick apartments,
    "projects," as if someone had made them
for school. Heat shimmered from roof-tops;
    as we pulled to the curb, my mother locked both
our doors, I heard a kitchen radio playing hymns,
    and saw in the red sun boys my own age
stripped to their briefs, alarmingly white
    against their skin, laughing while pummeled
by water from the corner hydrant they'd opened.

REUNION BANQUET, CLASS OF '79

"What happened to Charlotte Rampling?"—the vamp
and villainess of freshman year's remake,
Farewell, My Lovely. I can't recall the plot,
nor which boyfriend I went to see it with,

none villains. Freshman year, girls learn to drink;
we spent weekends bombed in years that followed,
often with those old boyfriends, some seated
in nearby chairs as we discuss *Three Women, Klute*

("poor Sutherland—what was the bomb that followed?"
"Fellini's *Casanova*"); Jane Fonda
changing women from fat dateless klutzes
to lean wives, marrying "that Turner guy,

a fellow Casanova before Jane."
Chinatown, Looking for Mr. Goodbar,
Diane Keaton ferrying from guy to guy
then killed. *Helter Skelter*, a TV movie

looked at with Chinese food and tepid beer,
that crammed dorm room (soph year? junior?), our knees
jellied. Hell, what's better than the movies
for filling gaps, for steering talk away

from this crammed corner's melodramas, its queens
of bad luck? Emma's three miscarriages—
"children fill a gap"; talk tries to veer away
but she tells us about her absent husband,

who blames their bad luck on her mom's DES,
how she spends Saturday nights now, fevered
by secrets she doesn't tell her husband:
chlymidia and one nostril scarred from coke,

for instance. *Saturday Night Fever!*
someone yelps, and Nan's atop the table—
clam sauce spotting her skirt, a Diet Coke
spilled—in the famous John Travolta pose;

someone yelps as Nan tips from the table,
as Layne prescribes a single mom's sanity:
sitcom repeats, like the John Travolta show
about the teacher, while she plugs into

tapes that prescribe ways to keep your sanity
while raising a small boy alone. Virginia
weeps—loudly—about the teacher who plugged her
senior year, and the men at the next table

rise to leave. "So long, boys," and then "virgins,"
sneers Laura, meaning none have been divorced,
not since senior year, when one at their table
tied the knot and wanted out weeks later.

The Deer Hunter. Most seated here are divorced,
and childless too. *Lipstick. Who'll Stop the Rain?*
I untie my knotted napkin, wanting out. It's late.
Woman under the Influence. Badlands.

"What happened to our apple charlottes?" Vanished,
like our lipsticked smiles, the bottles of wine.
We're women fluent with address pads and pens:
farewell, my lovelies. "I'll call, or write."

FOUCAULT IN VERMONT

No author for this fall landscape, nor signs
Of limits tested, except the fence just yards
From I-89, and a stray Holstein
Unfazed by traffic heading for the border.
How different from your time in California,
Those LSD trips at Zabriskie Point,
Warm nights spent cruising, or in Castro's bars
With studded whips and chains, implements
Not of love but knowledge: "to find God—
Or truth—in moments when the greatest pain
And pleasure are melted into one." De Sade
And de Chardin. The virus swarms your brain. . . .
But now this woolen hat. No melting here,
A state fist-fucked by winter every year.

DUPLEX NOIR

At dusk, stars fizzle in this landlocked sky
and TV screens turn blue, like smoke rising
from my neighbors' grill, smoke perfumed with meat
and already-spilled booze (they've bought enough):
bourbon for backslapping men, gin and tonic
for those first dates, white wine for moms who call

their sitters every hour. You haven't called;
my set darkens with Florida night sky,
Hurt and Turner sweating over tonics
slopped with rum, the tang of cut limes rising
as they plot to kill her husband. Enough—
I've seen *Body Heat* twice before, Matty

and Ned scheming to make Richard Crenna meat,
dead burned meat, between drinks and fucks and calls
dialed from pay phones. I've never had enough
of Florida, seared breeze and mackerel skies
at sundown, my sand-crusted knees rising
from castles left to watery tectonics

as my parents, gins lightly splashed with tonic,
picked at olives, cheese, cold sliced meats
and sang my name, their slurred voices rising
like the waves. Channel Eight: Lauren Bacall
in Martinique, monochromatic skies
and rum-runner Bogart, who's had enough

of Vichy thugs, who's never been loved enough,
as any dame can see. The movies are tonic
but addictive for little girls too shy
to play with boys, who cry into their meat
at dinners years later, when boys don't call
and when they do, when her father's shouts rise

and shake her bedroom walls. The volume rises
next door, where they've had more than enough,
the married and the single both. One call—
that's all it would take, and what's more tonic
than flesh on flesh? I could arrange to meet
you anytime. Stars vibrate in the sky,

now black above rising wires, trays of tonic
and leftover booze: they've burned enough meat
to call for pizza. Late news. No choice of skies.

YUCATAN, NOVEMBER

Calacas, the woman whispers, elbows our way past
stacked loaves of bread, past marigolds in earthen jars,
their dusty yellow stirring up last night's tequila:

five holiday shots, and the flowers on my room's walls
bloomed monstrously, their twisted stems coiling like snakes
before my eyes closed to sweaty, broken nightmares:

my grandmother's face metamorphosed six times a second
from flesh to skull then back. The woman's plump finger
points to a table, its *Especiale* sign;

at first I take her wares for dolls that my nieces
would love, though the paint on this figure's flower-cart,
that one's full tray, another's—a bishop's?—black miter,

is probably toxic with lead. A longer look,
and the *florista*'s face becomes a skull, the bar-maid's,
the churchman's; my god—he stands over a tiny coffin,

and when the woman presses a button, its skull,
joined to toothpick-sized bones, sits up and stares. How hard
to stare these—*mis calacas*—back into playthings

the living might clutch, as much effort as when,
sickened, but with a firm grip on my neck, I pressed
my lips to my grandmother's and imagined her

alive among drooped flowers, ready to kiss me back.
Head hurting worse, I open my wallet, hoping
to purchase escape, but the woman, bubbling vowels,

studies my shaky hands and pulls me through a door.
Am I being kidnapped, punished for not bringing
loved ones along with me? Here family's a religion,

worshipped even past *El Dia de Muertos*,
its flower-decked altars inviting forebears to enjoy
sugared bread and drinks like this, nearly as sweet

as my grandmother's iced tea: one sip and I'm less dizzy,
feel more at home, mildewed portraits of ancestors
surrounding me again. The dead lived among us

to judge and chasten, like stern-faced local saints;
making love for the first time in my heirloom bed,
I recalled my grandmother, kind but devout,

slept forty widowed years alone there, and I froze
as though a spell were cast. The woman takes my hand,
presses it onto a loaf: *pan de muerto*,

she whispers, and I hope not because she's possessed
of the second sight, sees in hungover pallor
what I've hardly tasted, rubbing my small mouth

in that funeral parlor's bathroom till the skin bled.
Pan de muerto crumbles on my tongue and I drain
the glass, a guest welcomed among marigolds,

welcomed but scarcely belonging; and once she's packed
two plastic bags with cut-rate *calacas*, blessed me
with *abrazos* that threaten to crack my bony ribs,

I look outside to the darkening sky, blazoned
by a jet's contrail, its twisted wisps of frozen vapor
ghosting the dusk and pointing the cold way home.

II

DELTA FUNERAL

I.

Starbursts, bouquets, wreaths of browning daisies,
 gaudy chrysanthemums in October's hues—
  pumpkin, winesap, mottled maize-yellow—

and a few wilted roses propped against the walls;
 nobody sitting on dozens of folding chairs;
  the talk so loud, the perfume so overpowering

in unseasonable heat, barely improved by the thrum
 of air conditioners jammed into windows,
  that I felt unhinged and dizzy, though not like

your brother, who'd hitchhiked from New Orleans,
 its steamy, mud-scented air and mean streets,
  not enough to hear voices in walls, or

to answer them. Your aunt's half-smile beneath
 the casket's open lid was mimicked instantly
  by all within earshot, trying not to stare.

2.

Graveside, mourners looked to see if her husband
     and your mother were crying. Tears a sign
          of weakness, worse, of rudely ignoring

the trouble they'd taken to come: straw hats,
     waxy pinks and reds of lipstick reflecting the sun,
          high heels, now sinking into cracked earth;

also the heavy flannel suits, handkerchiefs brought
     to mop necks. Yet true grief was present there,
          distracted with gestures and rites; while

your brother, dressed in a borrowed and baggy
     tweed jacket, dropped his voice to a hoarse growl,
          too low—mercifully—for anyone except

the family members positioned around him to hear,
     and talked of baseball, the cotton half-picked
          in surrounding fields, bad angels.

3.

At twenty, she pulled the trigger when her mare
    broke a leg, another time bludgeoned a rattler
        not six feet from where you played. More ladylike,

recent years spent tracing your family to a Frenchman
    who rode the Mississippi's silty currents,
        beginning with your uncle's Scots-Irish forebears,

believers in predestination, refusing free will.
    We'd try to track down your brother, we promised
        on that last weekend; she shut her eyes

and slept a night and a day, waking to walls
    reddened by sunset, wheezing phrases of a song
        she'd sung to you both as children, one blond

and docile, one fierce-eyed and dark, slipping
    through windows when he came to visit, and twice,
        for sheer meanness, unpeeling the wisteria

from her backyard trellis, their wing-shaped petals
    like the shadows she saw on walls at midnight
        and whispered to or prayed against, we couldn't tell.

INDEPENDENCE DAY

Charcoal fumes and smolders while my friend piles our plates
        with barbeque, his sauce
a family recipe and praised to the skies. This group's kids
        soon clamor for ice cream, which we skip to linger
                over beers in the hot twilight
circled by mosquitoes; when a hand waves one from my neck,
        I mistake the gesture
for my husband's, two chairs away, clasp that hand till someone
        cracks a joke and I blush,
                look away so fast I'm dizzied, long-known faces

suddenly too blurred to connect that one with twins,
        this one with a lost job,
another with ailing parents. Heat and bugs and voices
        whirl me from my own place in this humid circle,
                a whirl ridden to distant yards,
distant blocks—no, ridden farther, till the landscape changes
        and names scatter and dim.
Wasn't our country founded on such dreams of departure,
        dreams of new arrivals
                beneath brightly roman-candled skies? That woman

who's been sleeping for weeks at the mall's parking deck
        could tell her own version
over sandwiches and coffee, how her life downspiralled
        from its course of driving carpools and cooking meals,
                the comfort of a husband's touch, most nights.
Could tell how names like "wife" and "mom" were torn from her as
        quickly as I tear
"good Samaritan" from myself, who's made her story up—
        I didn't buy dinner
                for this woman and didn't even speak to her

when I fumbled with change among the shadowed cars.
        The sky's now turned jet-black,
and while the toddler twins are sleeping in their mother's arms,
        their friends fuss and whine, impatient for the fireworks.
                We carry chairs up the yard's slope
to see the spirals and rosettes and fans of tinted light
            explode through the darkness,
their patterns widening like the children's mouths, and brighter
            than Castor and Pollux,
        the Seven Sisters. Oh who's to say that nature

    and history, their unappeasing glut of facts,
            are children's best teachers,
that even these lines' fantasias won't widen my heart if
        I see the woman at the parking deck again?
                One twin wakes, and reaches toward
the sky's sweet artifice of flare and spark, which remembers
            a freedom-drunk midnight
long ago in a new world lit mostly by stars, their paths
            fixed and foretellable
        until those last blazing gestures toward extinction.

23 JOHNSON AVENUE, 1985

"Women, women, the whole house stank of them,"
Plath wrote in girlhood journals; I've mapped a drive
Through Wellesley streets reddened by fallen leaves
To find where she'd lived with Aurelia, dreamed
Of Daddy rising from Azalea Path,
Coming back to buy her pretty dresses.
Betrayed again, she honed words into scythes
That still draw blood: grayed Hughes arrives in Boston
The next month for a lawsuit; called "Murderer"
By those protesters frothing with old rage,
He's so handsome on TV my knees water.

    "Take us away from here," two daughters sang
In white suburban houses, dads absent,
Hoping to lure princes, sex our gaudy bait.

MAGI

Midnight neon flickers on the rain-sheened sidewalk,
    on that doorway's two women, their ebony hair
curled and intricate as the labyrinth described
    in *Stories from the Ancient World.* My father slows
until we're barely moving, the ice in his drink
    clinking on the dashboard above the greenish dials,
the radio's band of light. *Take a chance on romance*
    loud enough to reach that door, where one woman laughs

and starts a ragged duet. *A chance on romance*—
    I mouth the phrase with lips still sugar-tingling
from Christmas cookies eaten instead of supper,
    cookies till I'm glutted and offer the last star
to Anna Mae, bargaining for a late bedtime;
    soon my parents' key clicks in the door, wafting chill air
mingled with perfume and scotch-scent, and I'm allowed
    to ride along when he takes Anna Mae home, warm

in the backseat with her, streetlights disappearing
    as we approach the project where she lives. Curbside,
my father counts out bills then waves goodnight, turns up
    the radio—*take a chance*—and we speed downhill
and farther, till the city hurtles into view,
    multicolored strands of light shining from puddles
on the oily sidewalks, a mechanized Santa
    in a store window and a real one near the entrance,

his bell drawing coins from late passersby. Season
    of carols, tree decorations, being lifted
in my father's arms to place the gold crowning star.

No department store grandeur on the next few blocks,
just those pawn shops' iron grating padlocked in place,
    bars with steam-fogged windows and loud music spilling
from their doors as customers leave. The two women.
    What did I ask? *Fallen angels*, my father laughs,

mouth twisting like their ankles in spiky high heels
    just a few yards away, thin skirts and furry stoles
blown by December wind. One startles to see me
    kneeling in the backseat, hands pressed to the window,
and she looks angry as Anna Mae when I track
    muddy footprints across the rug, slamming her palm
on the car's hood. My father U-turns and my head bumps
    against the door, but I'm thinking about my book's

other stories. *For unto us this day is born*—
    didn't that scene take place at night too? We turn back
toward our neighborhood of clapboards and split levels,
    brown lawns puddled, red and gold and green lights hanging
like Babylon's gardens from naked dogwood trees
    and roofs, behind half-draped windows. Mother's sleeping;
Daddy forgets to read to me or hear my prayers,
    so I rehearse a new list for Santa: black wig,

high heels, a fur stole I'll let fall from one shoulder.
    How do angels fall, and does it hurt? Were the ones
we saw tonight there when Jesus was born, spike heels
    sunk in frigid sand as those wise men knelt before
the promised child, knowing their treasure—perfumed oils,
    gold coins—leaked and smudged as all the earth's best glories,
but their hands trembling to extend that bounty,
    their lips shaping prayers in return for divine love?

THE DOLLS

Those lolling china heads and rag-stuffed arms
Will never love us in return, said Rilke,
Whose mother dressed him like a girl, whose charms

Were sealed in letters for his distant harem.
"How dreadful," he wrote, "to spin our first silk"
For lolling china heads, for rag-stuffed arms

As plump as mine when young: the rich aroma
Of cakes rising, cream rising in whole milk.
My mother dressed me like a girl who'd charm

Her grown-up friends at teas, stroll through museums
And fall in love with statues, like Rilke,
Those lolling china heads and rag-stuffed arms

Turned to marble Apollos in his poems:
"Change your life." Easy for a god to talk—
No mother dressed him like a girl whose charms

Were pink and minor, who blinked with alarm
Whenever boys asked if she loved them back.
O lolling china heads and rag-stuffed arms—
Still I undressed, a girl with other charms.

TONSILLECTOMY

Mixed snow and sleet pock against the top-floor window
    and slick the empty streets below—*too dangerous*
        to drive, all expressways closed, too dangerous—

as a hospital nun bends to stroke the child's hair,
    her stitched throat packed with ice, eyes blinking past bedrails
        and that scatter of flakes to hold the night's slow whirl:

pine-scarred ridges circling downtown's lit skyscrapers,
    the molten flare and spark of late-shift furnaces;
        higher, monument to the ore that built this city,

iron Vulcan's bulk, larger than from the window
    by her bed at home, his snow-blurred fist holding
        an electric torch that beacons red when cars slam

and twist their metal into wreckage, or explode
    in fireballs shot to heaven. *Too dangerous—*
        a painful drowse, like last summer's fever dreams,

the sun resinous and white through her room's drawn shades,
    rays glittering the eyes of her stuffed animals.
        The nun adjusts this wall's crucifix, beads clicking

while she murmurs of Jesus, flocks of little ones,
    but the child wants to hear parts of *Mary Poppins*,
        her favorite bedtime book, soot-fogged London

and the nanny's medicine turned sweet cherry-red
    in glinting spoons, that night of the full moon,
        a zoo whose animals slipped magically through bars,

bright riffled pages of wolves and lions growling
    the paths below giraffes' elongated saunter,
        those bears and monkeys climbing the trees where vultures

plumped their feathers and the python hissed its song.
    No zoo trips for a year, riots making drives
        near downtown *dangerous, too dangerous*; and the child

wakes enough to hate her mother, who'd promised
    to bring ice cream, to read as many chapters
        as she wanted. The nun strokes her hair and says

that Jesus loves her, starched habit white as angels' wings
    on the walls of her Sunday School classroom:
        Son of God, Lamb of God, that voice fading to dreams

of late summer, how Vulcan's torch shone green
    through that maelstrom of debris, that church exploded,
        four girls her age found dead in the basement,

police dogs on TV, how much they looked like those wolves
    in Mary Poppins' zoo, for one night covering
        their fangs while lambs' pale fur brushed by them, lambs
            whose throats

they'd tear apart in seconds if prowling chill pine forests,
    spindly limbs cracked and broken with their frozen weight,
        green needles drifting down to the blood-spattered snow.

ALL THOSE PRETTY ONES

A girl's been raped in the snowbound northwest
By six grunge-clad assaulters who crooned Nirvana's
Early hit "Polly": its victim's flowered dress,
The flaring blowtorch & odd pleas for crackers
Are excerpted by the *Times*, delivered late
In mounting drifts. Quotes from the band's remains,
Though clotted with "you know" & "like," echo Yeats,
Who wondered if his play loosed rage in men
The British shot, if some, like Leda's twins,
Were born to breed terror. Below, wire photos
Of that collapsed zoo aviary in the Bronx,
Nineteenth century iron staves lying twisted
To ruin, gray-feathered birds pecking at snow.
Where will they fly, cramped wings, indifferent beaks?

JEHOVAH JIVEH

On the day before Easter, a furious rain swirls
        through this parking lot, so crowded that empty spaces
near the mall's entrance, its wind-jangled ferns, seem rare
    as miracles. The empty tomb, even Golgotha,

    would have drawn few believers in such gust-blown rain,
        ten needling days now of it, as though the sky's
about to swarm with angels, flame-robed and parted by
    a white horse bearing Christ, his name blood-inscribed

    on his left thigh. Was it first grade when we rehearsed
        for Armageddon, our dog tags clanking toward the basement
where we'd watched Kennedy's funeral? A black riderless horse.
    Black jets. Jackie veiled like Mary Magdalene

    in our class's play. Its six-year-old apostles,
        dressed in their fathers' bathrobes, knelt before a backdrop
of that empty grave, a mystery gentler than bombs
    or last Sunday's tornado, whirling through a church

    whose roof fell on the children's pageant, *Watch the Lamb*.
        Their small mouths closed on *Jehovah Jiveh*'s chorus—
"Sing God's Almighty Name"—to scream for heaven's mercy
    in a rain of wood and steel and glass. *Passion Week,*

    Jehovah Jiveh, Watch the Lamb—who watched for you,
        strayed angel, when your car tornadoed into metal shards
on that rain-slick road, when sirens parted the black night?
    Strayed angel and my heart's friend, you hymned our cities' streets,

those backdrops for hosts of lost souls; and you begged mercy
for them, begged even God's blazing face revealed
to limn world's end. The nightmares of bomb-shelter babies
are different, if no worse, than the kids' in this parking lot,

still damply clutched beneath their parents' umbrellas:
but should we have confused God with apocalypse,
with flattening winds and collapsed heaven and the earth lifting
one echo, *Jehovah*? Six children are buried

and you also on this day of wild needling rain,
and I won't ask about New Jersey's weather,
how many gathered, or how you looked in your beret
and high-necked dress. Or what flawed mortal songs were lifted

toward you, knowing none can rise high or loud enough.
Isn't this what you raged against, and tell me,
does it last beyond the grave, this ravening passion
to drown God's mighty thunder with our own scavenged hymns?

CHRISTMAS CALL

"Mama . . ., " she whispered, though I'm nobody's
mother. She sounded about my age.
The line cracked with the static
of long-distance: she was too far away
to be touched. But who's desperate

at four on a mild afternoon? Two weeks
until Christmas, almost sixty-five and sunny—
an autumn so warm the birds had gone
nowhere. We'd brought a tree home;
I'd unpacked decorations and planned

a night soon for the trimming—
I'd bake a fruitcake and mull wine.
We'd flattered ourselves with unhappy childhoods
and had been making it up ever since.
I thought I heard music—Rudolph?

White Christmas?—then again that one sound,
over and over, so softly no other
could know. I imagined a door locked
or a closet gone into, her voice muffled
by coats and stacked boxes, a husband

with fists cocked outside. I doubt my words
carried: the connection was bad.
Yet I pleaded to help her, call police
or a priest. At that moment I'd have let her
move in. A buzz caroled our cut-off;

I did nothing but sit there till dark.
After dinner it sleeted, we lit a fire,
and I drank a whole bottle of wine. Then later
that night, feeling naked and safe,
I said your name over and over.

PRODIGALS

On this darkened theatre's screen, a bike tire spins,
its spokes glittered by afternoon sunlight like that I'm blinking from,
       the bright sidewalk crowded with boys as they ran toward
the park; girls stared at the head shop's windows, perhaps dreaming

    of a bottle spinning amid candles: *Take me there.*
Take me with a kiss. I take a seat, still blinking, while Olivier,
       the movie's adored son, kisses *maman* goodbye
before pedalling toward the village, in his pocket

    a list of errands. She's long ignored her daughter,
Nadine, who takes revenge in her locked room with black candles and chants,
       who gets her wish when Olivier doesn't come back—
or not for six years, but now in greasy jeans, pockets bulged

    from franc notes made in Paris toilets. Soon she wakes,
dream-dazed, to find him in her bed. *If you left me again I'd die,*
       the mother says; and the girl thinks how only a fool
could believe this lying hustler will stay home in exchange

    for freshly-laundered Levis and a motorbike—
or is he really Olivier? Nadine slams her door as loudly
       as you did when you left, and now, months later, I dream
about my girlhood bedroom, whose door I locked to spend hours

    conjuring love scenes, staring at my lipsticked mouth
while dusk darkened the mirror. Or dream about the night a candle toppled
       and flamed the eyelet curtains, the night that boy, who'd climbed
across the sill to kiss me, leapt backward and ran

through the damp grass below. *He fell, he fell down those stairs,*
trying to run away—for six years, Olivier's lain buried
        in the village pervert's cellar, and the young poseur,
    who discovers this by accident, throws a punch at him

        then leaps onto his motorbike, in hours blurting
the entire story to the Parisian detective who "found" him
        in the first place, happy to reunite a mother
    with a runaway who just might be her son. The camera

        cuts quickly to her—*if you left me again I'd die*—
face motionless and slack with weeping, supported by Nadine,
        her mouth smudged with lipstick, *papa* absently nervous,
    as the fake Olivier strides toward the kitchen table

        and relights that face with love. A few last credits roll
before the screen darkens like the twilit park, where I've locked my bike
        to a sign that forbids loitering—*I will arise*
and go—and reflects a woman who escapes to matineés,

        those easy transports, from a half-empty house,
but who wants only your returned, prodigal kisses, a woman
        whose ears hum—*take me there, take me*— as I nudge
    the kickstand, begin to pedal in pink suspended light.

III

DESCANT

Beneath the sidewalk's iron grates, those ice-slicked portals
                  to an underworld of trains
            whose tunnelled rush became a woman's voice—
how easy, in that long Manhattan winter, to hear Persephone
      mourning sunlit earth and its maternal warmth,
                  also mourning the taste
            of those sweet red seeds. How easy now to hear
                  her whisper through chill wind,
      a thousand miles south from a man who whispered *love*

      deep in his throat as snow-pocked obsidian windows
                  turned violet then crimson.
            Beyond my empty classroom's rattling panes,
a tree clings to its few last gaudy leaves; from the parking lot
      of this girls' school, some muted rock-and-roll rises
                  with forbidden smoke.
            Who wants to study when her winter prom
                  is just a week away?—
      by then more letters will crowd my gradebook's pages

      in a well-ordered train. But what chaotic gods
                  the heart has always worshipped;
            and would my students gape in disbelief
if I told them how quickly I undress when someone whispers *love,*
      shed my clothes on floors that seem to cleave
                  beneath my feet? Outside,
            those almost-naked trees surround a fountain
                  like the mythic one
      that virgin goddess vanished by; its chitoned girls

shyly bend their heads as Cupid grins and clutches
his bow, graffiti scrawled
on one plump leg: *Virginia* ♥ *Harry*.
Aren't all women Persephone, lost to the dark allure of sex
between parted sheets, waiting for flesh to warm them
while invisible mothers
tear their long robes, cry to the chilling earth
and cloudy deaf heaven?
Clasping that man's body, once I whispered the name

of a daughter as longed-for, and even untouched,
as the body mourned
by any woman who's lost herself again,
a daughter whose first sounds would silence the parking lot's traffic
and rustling trees outside, a daughter like me
whose cry said *I'll love you*
till trees turn red with fruit and dying leaves,
till your sweet eyes are closed
with pennies; I'll leave you for love for love for love.

HISTORY

It's blood, and generals who were the cause,
Shadows we study for school. In Nashville, lines
Of a Civil War battle are marked, our heroes
The losers. Map clutched in one fist, my bike
Wobbling, I've traced assaults and retreats,
Horns blowing when I stopped. The South's hurried
And richer now; its ranch-house Taras display
Gilt-framed ancestors and silver hidden
When the Yankees came, or bought at garage sales.
History is bunk. But who'd refute that woman
Last night, sashaying toward the bar's exit
In cowboy boots to drawl her proclamation?—
"You can write your own epitaph, baby,
I'm outta here—*comprendo?*—I'm history."

THE OLD SLAVE MARKET, CHARLESTON
—May, 1992

The cracked bricks have loosened with age, with two earthquakes
    rivalling any that collapse skyscrapers elsewhere;
with twenty hurricanes, the last whose devastation
    left in its wake scaffolds around the pastel walls
of stately columned houses and breeze-front piazzas;
    around the steeple of St. Michael's, the oldest church—
or is that St. Philip's? Words like "first" and "oldest"
    spark arguments here, though surely not on this gift

of a spring afternoon. I finger baskets made
    by plaiting sea-grasses, an art which may die out
with women who sell in this tourist-crammed market
    on weekends, weaving new holders for bread-loaves,
dried flowers, or jewelry. "Basket ladies," they're called,
    & a few feet away hang Christmas ornaments
that resemble them: black wooden silhouettes
    wearing real bandanna headrags. A founding father

gave this land to the city, a permanent marketplace
    for anything *but* slaves, natives are quick to tell you.
Its name comes from the field hands used for hauling barrels
    of rice & indigo, ripe-to-exploding peaches
& tomatoes, from plantation wagons; or stacking
    cotton bales between brick pillars while the auctioneer
took bids, his voice echoing through salt-heavy air.
    Now, two thousand miles distant, the glass shatters

from Los Angeles storefronts built to weather nothing
    but daily traffic, the quick glances of passersby
en route to bus stops or street corner deals, at worst

the usual burglaries, with metal grating drawn
at closing time, with alarm bells & triple-locks.
        "Our first multiracial riots," a newsman proclaimed,
voiced-over shots of whites, blacks, & Hispanics
        who carried armfuls of wrenches & clocks, sparkplugs

& a butcher's fat hams. They rushed through streets littered
        with broken liquor bottles, foam-spewing cans of beer
dropped by those running from police or store owners.
        Or each other. Lawn sprinklers, cartons of Twinkies
& cigarettes, rhinestone necklaces in gutters,
        on sidewalks, in hands trembling with adrenalin
& greed. The woman's hands before me are steady,
        sinewed from generations of slaves' hardscrabble,

the continuing lineage of taking in laundry,
        diapering white babies in bay-windowed nurseries,
polishing silver to grace meals eaten off china
        passed down from mother to daughter, except for
those dinner plates dropped too hard in sinks, tea cups
        allowed to smash on floors always swept clean before
the bus ride home. Ignoring signs above her cashbox,
        her newspaper folded beside it, the woman lights

a cigarette, tosses the match too near the grass
        piled at her feet, as if wanting conflagration,
as if wanting to see huge flames weave their bright orange
        & red together, then lift their work toward a sky
today unclouded with judgment, perhaps waiting
        another century before darkening with flood-rains,
before loosing winds which may or may not blow
        these famed houses & churches, these old brick walls, down.

HOUND DOG

Lapin au poivre, at your fork's plunge so lavishly pungent
      my mouth waters in this West Village restaurant
      whose tablecloth we've already spotted with wine
           and bits of bread. Long since moved back to native ground,
I'm foolhardy with nostalgia on these yearly visits
      & last night walked late to that spotlit marble arch,
         despite dealers crooning by the vine-snaked columns,
the pursesnatchers & worse. Just like those a decade ago—
      during lectures on tragedy, my gaze would drift

to the windows, & once it was stopped by what might have been
      a mugging, what might have been a lovers' quarrel,
      the unluckier dropping on one knee to clutch
         a torn heart. Ten years of dinners & I've told you
this story before, how I didn't even raise my hand,
      too unsure of what I'd witnessed, too worried you
        & the others in that classroom would interpret
such alarm as a rube's hysteria. I'm alarmed now
      when you push away your glass & meat-spattered plate

to take my hand, our fingers mingling until a dropped tray
      explodes with china: the moment's repaired with jokes
      about future embraces made leaning on canes,
         about how our ringed fingers will be too gnarled to tear
each others' clothes to shreds. How I've missed you, & this city,
      its neon-charged, perilous erotics of flux—
      ELVIS LIVES, reads a graffitied store grate we pass
on Waverly Place, vainly signalling cabs; back at home,
      Presley-sightings are common, my favorite claimed by

a woman who spotted him among extras when *The Firm*
was being shot. *I'll take the King over Tom Cruise*
any day, she said on the news. Her slackened skin
overlaid the face of the high-schooler she'd been
forty years before, brain & underwear moist, tears streaking
her plump cheeks as she tilted back her throat to yowl.
Others ripped off bras inky with their phone numbers,
shorts with hotel room keys in their pockets, & hurled them toward
the spotlit snaking pelvis, the curled swollen lips

that crooned versions of a dithyramb always translated
as *come away, come away with me.* Is that why
New York is so crowded with throngs who land then stay,
who hear those primal chords in the city's sirens
& blaring horns, in the music vibrating downtown clubs
before dance-frenzied souls drift homeward, paired at dawn?—
what glorious splintering comes when we lose ourselves
in another, though sometimes "I love you" sounds dangerous
as "your money or your life." A cab finally slows

& farewell tears sting my eyes, although I smile too
as the opening phrase of "Hound Dog" crashes through
the cab's window. *You ain't never caught a rabbit—*
of course Orpheus drove those country housewives mad,

dancing & holding that lyre just out of their hungry reach,
like your fingers still held an inch from the window;
of course they wanted to tear apart the singer,
tear him to bloody bits, so he couldn't leave them alone
with the music of their savagely pulsing hearts.

GEORGIA PILGRIMAGE

Crowds thin as winter nears, as the trees lift
    their black and twisted limbs toward leaden skies
        that today show no signs of Mary's face,

"sad but so pretty," said the local farmwife
    whose sightings drew thousands last summer,
        church busses unloading the sick and lame,

those failed by love, in humid air some swore
    was perfumed with roses. My nose prickles
        at the stale grease that films this diner's booth,

the framed clippings and photos hung above it
    of a child crowned just last month in a pageant
        when her flaming baton act—I crane to read

small print—"dropped the crowd to its knees."
    A waitress fills my cup, and, shyly beaming,
        says she coached her child's routine all year,

curled the ringlets that halo those pink cheeks.
    They're plump as the cortisone-swollen ones
        of this state's most famous author, whose face rises,

her body slumped on crutches, from my book,
    already sticky but wreathed with coffee-steam
        in this refuge from wind, those now-famed skies

empty except for leaves. Leaves splotched the road
    that leads back here then to another farm,
        where Flannery lived with peacocks and her mother,

whose beatitudes—"pretty is as pretty does"—
    echo through that story of a crippled girl,
        acid-tongued and frumpy till she's smitten

with a Bible salesman who steals her wooden leg.
    There's enough light to reach the place by sunset,
        and the waitress, who took a trip there before

she left high school, bends in a perfumed cloud
    and smooths a spotted menu, drawing a map
        to where O'Connor stood at twilight, watched

her peacocks spread their tails in a strutting pageant
    through the red-clay yard, screeches echoing
        toward each other like electrified applause;

where she prayed—*Mother of God*—that her loneliness
    be warmed by more than immaculate beauty,
        those thousand blue and green eyes winking among

black feathers like stars, beauty that requires
    incense and flowers, prayers that soar sky-high
        as it knocks us to unlovely, creaking knees.

"THE HOMELESS IN AMERICA"

—photographic exhibit at the Parthenon,
Centennial Park, Nashville

Black-and-white, their faces and clothes
could come from any era
I've read about in school or seen blazoned
on late-night TV. Two women
wear bedspreads as shawls. A man washes
his armpits with water collected
in someone's cracked bowl and uses
a hamburger wrapper to dry them.

Most seem religious: they point skyward
or to Bibles hung onto from childhood;
one opens hers to a family grouping
of haloed angels and saints. Another
says in the caption that she lifted
her copy from a Birmingham shelter
but doesn't think Jesus would mind.
She knew no one was looking.

A New Jersey woman covers her son's legs
with trashbags: they've been sleeping
on benches for weeks. His hair's caked
and matted, still she tries to smooth it,
her cracked fingers sorting his miniature
dreadlocks and probably finding lice.
Is this our Pietà? Is this child
even alive?—his mother's half-smile

so naked and craving I imagine
she's mad. And dead sons are the norm here—
a fake marble Niobe and sad kneeling Thetis,

Andromache tearing her breast.
The largest statue is of Pallas Athene,
all forty-two feet of plaster
and drapery. Her hands are the size

of my chest; one carries a spear.
She had no use for husbands or children,
a real Daddy's girl, inventing our romance
with law and banishing Furies. Beyond
are the too-perfect columns,
an expanse of green park. The gods,
like the poor, are hard to look at
and will be with us always.

MULTIPLE EXPOSURE

Triangulation, he screeches, almost a caricature
of the sleazy underworld goon—but limp-wristed,

wearing a skewed fright wig & diagonal slashes
of eyebrow pencil—in Stone's *JFK,* charting figures

in a New Orleans flat to be transferred to Dallas
that autumn, on streets instead of a blackboard:

two audiences watch his fingers slice through air
& are hushed, believing. How clear it all seems

in slow motion, with jump-cuts & spliced footage:
Kennedy clutches his throat an instant before

the back of his head explodes; Jackie crawls over
the trunk wanting help or escape, & threeway crossfire

is a sure thing—knoll, building, fence—just as
your hand strokes my breast & I remember another's

hand, close my eyes & confuse your hair's texture
with his, the shapes of eyebrows, parted mouths,

curves & rhythms of hips. Outside a low sun reddens
the sky; two neighborhood boys pelt a third with rocks

while he gives them the finger & bicycles away,
imagining cheering crowds, front-page revenge on those

who call him *fag, pussy,* accuse him of *eating come.*
He'll get them. He's got all the angles figured.

BODIES

Low-angle shots show Viv, Eliot's hormone-plagued first wife,
sunk to her knees and scrubbing, scrubbing blood-stained hotel sheets
while her husband walks along the beach, crowded with housewives
and families on holiday. He wishes his new wife
were like those singing mermaids he wrote poems about in college,
poems he later recited Camside to court his future wife,
eyes needy in the flashback as when she becomes his wife,
as when she's pronounced "morally insane," drunk on ether
and raving about thrice-monthly periods and saints. Either
you take his side or you take hers: wives sympathize with wives,
usually, husbands with husbands, but I fell in love
with Eliot during freshman year, read "Prufrock" and loved

every last word. Getting pregnant the first time you make love
is awful luck: my roommate hid in clothes like a fat housewife's,
spent five months drunk before she finally told her ex-lover
and me, who took the Pill each time I thought I was in love.
A shot and—I'll call her Ruthie—writhed on clinic sheets,
writhed as I read to her the bedstand's *From Russia with Love*
and *Modern Poets,* read to myself *Saying No and Love;*
and British spies and Prufrock and freak pregnancies collaged
with punk blared from next door, where kids from another college,
in that town we'd come to by bus, heard the death of love
and God and maybe Queen Elizabeth screeched by either
Sid Vicious or Johnny Rotten, or maybe both. "Ether

is contraindicated for your friend's procedure; ether
lessens the contractions and the fetus won't expel, love"
a nurse said on that night's first rounds, the full moon etherous
and clouding over in the window pane. Smell of ether—
no, Lysol—and Ruthie's sweat. Was Nancy Spungeon a wife,
or a girlfriend, when her nags sabotaged that haze of ether

Sid wrapped around himself, a heroin drift etherous
and shared like the Chelsea Hotel's cigarette-scarred sheets,
till he stabbed her dead? I read "Prufrock" aloud, smoothed those sheets,
fed Ruthie ice-chips till she finished screaming in the calm ether
of the recovery room, dark as that bar near our college
where the father cried and gave me cash: "Three years of college

and she thought a baby could be wished away?" Back at college,
Ruthie moved to another dorm; by the next year, either
she'd lost contact with me or vice versa, and I left college
for more school, to study those poems Eliot wrote at college
on erotic martyrs like Sebastian and the arrows he loved.
Now Viv dies in the asylum: I'm pulled from friends at college
to recall scenes from that other movie, just after college,
its scenes razored by Nancy's whine—she was a perfect wife,
if you live in hell and want some company, like a wife.
The two films twine with that clinic, the club's kids from college
who spewed cheap beer, Ruthie's *why not you?* muffled by sheets
as I left at twelve to buy cigarettes and stand in sheets

of rain like tonight's, peering through the door at a torn sheet
emblazoned with a safety-pinned Queen Liz, at a collage
of pulsing acrid spotlights, of beer and spit and blood in sheets.
"I'm not an animal," rose Sid's dazed choral leer, sheeting
the words in cut-throat fury. "And I'm not a discharge, either"—
"I'm an abortion." Eliot sent his friend Aiken a sheet
of the *Times* once, red-circling words like "mucus," "bloody sheets,"
but this after he'd renounced Viv and her half-mad love.
Aiken's left out of tonight's film, which, like London, I love,
though I'm travelling alone, sleeping chilled by nylon sheets.

On the late bus, a punk trio—husband, toddler, wife—
nuzzle each other's spiky hair; he kisses his wife,

who's given birth to more than rage and pain. Both of us wives
just after graduation, Ruthie, and I sent you lace sheets
but missed your wedding, write each year in care of the college.
This scrawled postcard will say there aren't any mermaids here, either,
but the punk husband's singing—I swear—a lullaby, with love.

STORY HOUR

Near the parking lot, a few last red leaves swirl—
catch me, catch me if you can—toward twilit skies
scarred with late autumn's frozen bits of cirrus.
Or are they contrails? A jet's roar lifts my eyes—

catch me, catch me if you can—toward twilit skies
and I walk too close to a kid-crammed car,
which swerves and tailspins. Snow White lifted her eyes,
still drugged with sleep, for a smitten prince;

but walking too close to a kid-crammed car,
my eyes updrifting with those red swirled leaves,
is dangerous. Like sleeping with a smitten prince—
but that's a fairy tale. Here's a true story,

one that little kids, driven home through leaves
from neighborhood libraries, shouldn't hear—
it's a scary tale—though this true story
ends with justice done: last night at a bar

near the library, my friend said she'd just heard
that the man who's raped ten local women
has been arrested, been locked behind bars.
Married, a father of twins, he lives nearby,

this man who's raped ten local women
(I've seen him around, mowing his backyard
or tossing balls for kids who live nearby);
he's described and named by the newspaper

I found this morning in our frost-flecked yard,
the grass like crystal. My friend talked of his wife,
also described and named in the newspaper,
then sipped her red wine. "She'll never be the same."

We looked at men and talked of being wives,
and lipstick, but kept other secrets. Last week
a man I can't forget said he felt the same,
looking at me in this library parking lot

(I've kept secret about this since last week)
as he did when looking at old pictures
of his ex, who'd worked at the library
and lived with him but without warning moved

to Colorado, which she'd looked at in pictures.
My friend, an alarmist, once said rapists
often stalk victims at libraries or movies.
But in this parking lot, that man's eyes shone lonely,

and I've walked back here every day. A rapist,
or a prince, who might return with a kiss?
This empty parking lot now shines lonely
with the half-swallowed sun, cars bound for home.

Should I hope he'll return with a kiss,
having trailed me here? A jet's roar lifts my eyes.
I'm wearing red lipstick, which I don't at home.
Catch me, catch me if you can, beneath twilit skies.

CHORALE

A sack of rotting apples dizzied Schiller's brain
       as he wrote, drunk on scent
and words, those now-unread plays, even *Wilhelm Tell* recalled
       only for its hero, whose arrows sang through air
             to find their red, heart-shaped targets.
My friend fills her syringe while I search for my car keys, turn
       to see the needle plunged
into her left thigh: "diabetes," she tells me

       en route to the café, means "siphon," the body
             melting down to water;
"mellitus" describes the sweet smell of the patient's urine.
       Pouring vials near an anthill was the ancient test
             for this disease; if the ants swarmed,
the prognosis was coma, followed by that deepest sleep,
       sugar levels risen
so high they thrum the blood to stasis. In August,

       when her lover went back home to his wife, my friend
             skipped one shot, two, skipped meals
to binge on twelve-hour naps, waking to nibble candy
       and hear, through the thin walls, an elderly neighbor
             playing sonatas. "Ode to Joy,"
Schiller's most famous work, though we nearly lose the lyric
       in Beethoven's grand chords,
the 9th symphony composed after his ears closed

       to all but music, as my friend's eyes closed to all
             but the black-winged angel.
That neighbor heard no footsteps or rattle of plates for days,
       worried enough to call and ask if I had keys:
             even outside the dark bedroom

we smelled the perfume of—roses? No, fruity and cloying,
        like a sack of apples
    left to rot. The ambulance crew filled a syringe

        on arrival, trained for signs of blood-sugar soared
            sky-high. "Dumb thing to do,"
my friend says, scanning the menu and sipping Diet Coke,
        and I'm not sure if she means the man or her try
            at self-destruction, drowning
in a forbidden rapture. The last time I fell in love
        I played Beethoven
    so loud that pictures trembled and china rattled

        its shelves, *Chorale's* strings and winds and horns confirming
            that joy—*freude, freude*—
is what we all desire, that while deep-kindled by the scent
        of hair, or the brief feathery touch of a hand,
            or the sight of a parted mouth,
desire arrows its way into the brain till flesh and mind
        become as one, singing
    our unrequitable ache to drown in sweetness.

ABOUT THE AUTHOR

Diann Blakely, who published previously as Diann Blakely Shoaf, was born in Alabama and educated at Sewanee, Vanderbilt, NYU, and Vermont College. Her first collection, *Hurricane Walk,* appeared in 1992 and was named one of the year's ten best poetry books by the *St. Louis Post-Dispatch.* A two-time Pushcart winner, Blakely currently serves as a poetry editor of *Antioch Review* and co-editor of *Each Fugitive Moment*, a collection of essays on the late Lynda Hull. She has received citations from the University of Chicago and Vanderbilt University for excellence in teaching.